Working the System

Dr. Federica Robinson-Bryant

Working the System

Published by Denotion Research Group
www.DenotionResearch.com

Cover & Illustrations by Tullip Studio

ISBN:
978-1-958634-41-7 (2nd edition print)
978-1-958634-14-1 (1st edition print)
978-1-958634-15-8 (eBook)

Printed in United States
2nd Edition

Dedication

This book is dedicated to my incredibly supportive parents,
who instilled in me the most important rule of all: "do it anyway."
In life, there will be problems to solve and systems to navigate.
When you face an obstacle, don't shy away. Just do it anyway!

When I was your age, I liked trying new things,
often excited, but sometimes full of doubt.
I usually found value in experiencing something different,
and sought opportunities to grow and figure things out.

One time I worked at one of the largest defense contractors, supporting a program to refurbish helicopters.

As technology evolved and new standards emerged, those cockpits became the new technology's early adopters. **MODERNIZATION** they called it.

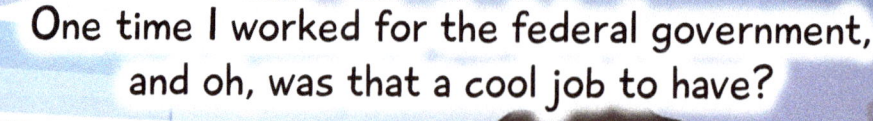

One time I worked for the federal government, and oh, was that a cool job to have?

-80℃

I worked on training systems- old and new, involving VR goggles, weapons, and simulators too, to ensure the soldiers were prepared.

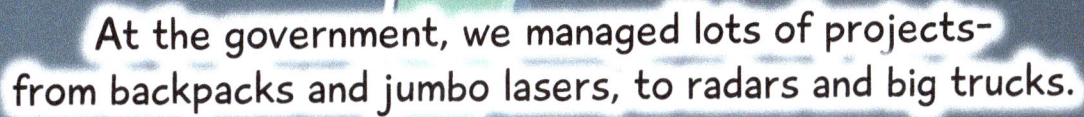

At the government, we managed lots of projects—
from backpacks and jumbo lasers, to radars and big trucks.

We worked with different teams within and outside our organization
to realize new systems and retire others when their time was up.
OBSOLETE they would call those.

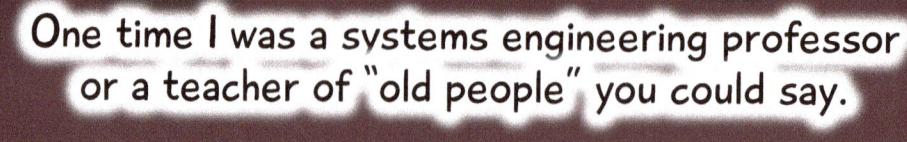

One time I was a systems engineering professor or a teacher of "old people" you could say.

For that I earned as much education as I could, achieving the title of Doctor along the way.

As a professor I was able to do many things.
I taught all kinds of stuff:
from engineering to systems to even how people think...
I've taught that to simply know is never enough.

My students lived all over the world,
and came from many different backgrounds.

From engineers, to pilots, to aspiring astronauts-
oh, the extraordinary adventures they've found.

Along this journey, I have written many works.
I have traveled and met all kinds of leaders.
I have shared ideas, heard ideas, and created new ones,
while turning many naysayers into believers.

Travel, you ask? Why yes indeed—
from domestic,
to other countries,
and different continents.

No matter what role I seemed to hold,
I learned new things, new cultures, and developed new interests.

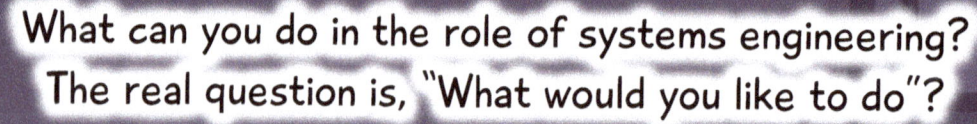

What can you do in the role of systems engineering?
The real question is, "What would you like to do"?

Because the only real boundaries that exist when you choose
this field, are those created by you.

Can you direct a top secret, artificial intelligence project?

Yes indeed, that's working the system!

Vocabulary

Adopt

Architect

Artificial Intelligence

Astronaut

Autonomous

Background

Boundaries

Context

Culture

Defense Contractor

Design

Domain

Dynamic

Emerge

Engine

Engineering

Entrepreneur

Evolve

Extraordinary

Federal Government

Field

Footprint

Idea

Interactions

Vocabulary

Interest

Invent

Leader

Modernization

Obsolete

Opportunity

Organization

Performance

Profession

Professor

Program

Project

Realize

Refurbish

Retire

Robotics

Simulator

Standards

System

Systems Engineer

Team

Technology

Training System

Virtual Reality